BÔ YIN RÂ

THE BOOK
ON
HUMAN NATURE

Bô Yin Râ is the author of a cycle of thirty-two works, titled *Hortus Conclusus* (*The Enclosed Garden*). The following other works of that cycle are available in English translation:

The Book on the Living God

The Book on Life Beyond

The Book on Happiness

The Book on Solace

The Wisdom of St. John

The Meaning of This Life

Spirit and Form (forthcoming)

Also available is a brief biography of the author and a general introduction to his works, titled *About My Books, Concerning My Name, and Other Texts*.

BÔ YIN RÂ
(J. A. SCHNEIDERFRANKEN)

THE BOOK
ON
HUMAN NATURE

TRANSLATED BY
B.A. REICHENBACH

BERKELEY, CALIFORNIA

English translation © 2000 by B. A. Reichenbach

Eric Strauss, Publisher & Editor

All rights reserved.

For permission to quote or excerpt, write to:
THE KOBER PRESS
2534 Chilton Way
Berkeley, California 94704

email: koberpress@mindspring.com

This book is a translation from the German of the second edition of
Das Buch vom Menschen by Bô Yin Râ (J.A. Schneiderfranken), first
published in 1928. The copyright to the German original is held by
Kober Verlag AG, Bern, Switzerland.

Printed in the United States of America

Library of Congress Control Number: 00-131087

International Standard Book Number: 0-915034-07-7

Typesetting and design by Irene Imfeld, Berkeley, CA

Book cover after a design by Bô Yin Râ

ACKNOWLEDGMENT

For patiently examining the various
drafts of this translation, and for her many
thoughtful comments and suggestions,
the writer gratefully expresses
his indebtedness to

Alice Glawe

CONTENTS

INTRODUCTION

"In seeking God, the *human being* must become the point of your departure, lest God remain a stranger to your soul forever."

These words I wrote some years ago in *The Book on the Royal Art.*

Today, I do not think there could be a more fitting introduction to the present *Book on Human Nature.*

TOGETHER WITH *The Book on the Living God* and *The Book on Life Beyond*, this *Book on Human Nature* is to form a trilogy; for even though each book is in itself complete and independent in perspective, they all remain connected by an inner bond and many passages will thus elucidate each other.

Yet such related explanations can only deepen the impression that these words will have upon the reader's soul.

May, then, *The Book on Human Nature* likewise come into the hands of those who are no longer unacquainted with those other works.

May it find the hearts that are in need of what it has to give: the souls who are prepared and willing to receive its message!

ALTHOUGH I RECOGNIZE that what I have to say can easily, alas, be misconstrued, I nonetheless regard it as important to state here very clearly that, like all my books, the present work as well was written in fulfillment of accepted obligations, wholly in agreement with the *Elders* of the spiritual brotherhood to which I, as a member, owe everything I have to give.

The insights offered in these pages are the spiritual heritage, preserved through the millennia, of those who, since the dawn of human life on earth, have been appointed eternally to guard the sacred flame whose radiant light originates within the Light of the Beginning.

As for ourselves, we only seek to share with others what long ago we, too, had once received, in order that, through us, it be conveyed again, both to the present and to future generations.

We do not claim to be the *authors* of these teachings.

Nor, for that matter, are we teaching "doctrines." Our aim, instead, is to transmit results of our *practical experience* within the worlds of the eternal Spirit, the world whose forms are living light, the realm from which descended every human soul embodied on this earth.

And so, this *Book on Human Nature*, too, will lead into the radiant world of Spirit.

To many, this may seem a contradiction, because they have not yet considered that the spiritual, the ultimately *real* human being is no less an emanation, born of love, by male and female energies within the world of radiant spiritual substance, than the human mortal's earthly organism is the issue of the physical erotic union of man and woman in the realm of matter.

But those who would discern the human being's *spiritual* reality, and thus begin to know themselves, must do so in the human spirit's home. Their quest must be directed toward the paths on which the soaring heights can be ascended within whose realm the timeless human being's *spiritual* organism has its roots. Mortal senses cannot ever apprehend that realm, nor will the earthbound human mind become aware of its existence other than by sensing the effects which spiritually generated causes establish here on earth.

As long as our concept of the "human being" comprises no more than that being's mortal form on earth, we see before us mainly a discordant *animal*; discordant, since that being is not satisfied with living merely as an animal, but can evidently be inspired to experience matters that transcend the animal's potential; discordant, in particular, because it is prevented, precisely by those energies, which lie beyond the animal's capacities, from innocently savoring its creature life in earthly pleasures, undisturbed by any sense of guilt.

Above all else it thus is necessary to discern and overcome the misconception that the

human being is no more than the material creature we on earth regard as "man."

ONE CANNOT BLAME a thinking individual, espe-
cially not one who has lost faith in human
nature, if he can only muster an ironic smile
when reading the majestic words that call the
human being the "image of God"—if his idea
of human nature does not extend beyond the
purely mortal aspect of that being.

Indeed, to call the human being "the image
of God," would be the height of folly, if the
author of those words had been referring merely to that being's earthly form.

Whoever first envisioned that comparison was
either a pathetic fool—or an enlightened sage,
who had discerned the all-encompassing reality of Man within the Spirit's world.

WHAT THE CONCEPT "human being" must in fact
comprise, if it would signify eternal Man as
such, not merely one of Man's innumerable
emanations—both in the spiritual world, as
well as in the universe experienced through
material senses—is shown you in the present
Book on Human Nature.

I trust you will no longer think the sage's word so foolish once you fully comprehended what I have to say.

You then will understand the meaning of the venerable ancient text declaring, "In the likeness of God the Elohim created Man."

And, thus, you will no longer search for mankind's first progenitors on this material planet; for you will know that what you thought was "early man" should more correctly be described as the primeval *animal*, from which evolved the subtler kind of creature that now provides the human being with a body as a tool, so that the human individuation may experience its existence in the domain of physical reality.

Again, you will no more "despair" of humankind, having grasped that everything you used to look upon as miserable, small, and wretched in the creature known on earth as "man" is typically the nature-driven and, therefore, inescapable assertion of the mortal animal's existence—whose energies the timeless human spirit seeks to use as means to manifest its own eternal self—but which is often more resistant to the spirit's will than the latter's power can surmount in earthly life.

Other things you will begin to see as unavoidable results of "friction," caused by the collision of such profoundly unlike forces.

Nor will you ever fantasize again about creating "paradise" on earth, having understood that not even the earth-born human *animal*, which is to serve the *human spirit* in this world of matter, could ever find its "heaven" in this life. The human spirit, on the other hand, had long ago possessed its heaven: before it thrust itself into the realm of physical creation, where now the animal, in which it is embodied, needs to lend the human spirit its own energies if that spirit is to find the way that leads it back into that heaven.

Count it as a blessing if, having read the expositions that you now have in your hands, you came to understand that you yourself are, in reality, a being that descended from the human spirit's timeless home, not just the more developed animal to which you find yourself so closely bound that until now you may not even have perceived it as a thing distinguished from yourself, a force in opposition to your real nature.

And blest you are, indeed, if then you raise yourself with all your strength and henceforth only seek your nature's highest purpose. For you have far too long been mired in your depths, and far too often have your hands groped through miasmas of uncertainty, where they had searched in vain for what they thought they might discover.

I want to see you full of confidence in your own strength.

You can no longer feel disdain for your own nature once you begin to recognize, however faintly, that nothing in you justifies disdain—except what you yourself have made contemptible: through false interpretation.

From that day on you shall no more debase yourself by making common cause with low pursuits.

You henceforth shall no longer strive for what is base within your nature.

You will, instead, become a resolute "insurgent," one who rises up and tears himself out of the clinging mud that covers all the crowded common roads.

Being free, you then shall scale the rock-hewn path that, in yourself, will lead you to the snow-capped peaks you find within.

There you shall come face to face with your eternal nature: a timeless human self, once more alive in mankind's lasting home, abiding in the Spirit.

CHAPTER ONE

THE MYSTERY ENSHROUDING MALE AND FEMALE

ABIDING IN THE DEPTH of the Eternal Origin: within the Spirit that continuously generates itself, and, in itself, all Being, all Existence—eternally concealed in the unfathomed source from which arises all of Being, all Reality that is becoming manifest—there lies enshrined the mystery surrounding *male* and *female*.

To bridge the gap that hinders mental comprehension, thinking minds will use the concept "spirit" as an abstract essence, pure and wholly "absolute." In fact, however, such an essence, conceived as purely *absolute*— detached, existing only in and for itself, immovably at rest—never did exist, does not exist today, nor ever could exist in all eternity.

Those who view this mental construct as objective truth put undue trust in speculative thinking. They have not yet begun to grasp that logical deductions cannot ever reach beyond the limits which determine every concept that is still within the laws which govern all of human thought.

The Spirit's infinite reality, however, is subject to no law excepts its own. And no attempt to fathom that reality through logical analysis can ever hope to comprehend it.

Embracing its own substance in itself, the Spirit of Eternity continuously generates its own existence through the aeons—becoming its own Father and own Mother—because eternal Spirit is in essence *male* and *female*.

Yet from that first self-revelation in the Origin, *Male* and *Female* in the Spirit continue to engender and bring forth, without beginning, without end, the Human Being dwelling in the Spirit. And they engender and bring forth that timeless Human "after their own image," in the likeness of the Spirit's *male* and *female* nature, reflecting the originally manifested oneness of bipolar life in union.

All things perceived as manifest reality: all the suns and worlds throughout the spiritual, as well as the material universe, which we experience through our mortal senses, *everything* is the "creation"—insofar as its appearance is perceptible reality—of that eternal Human, originating in the Spirit. That whole "creation," thus, is likewise testimony manifesting Male and Female in the Spirit.

This first, primordial Human Being of the Spirit is begot and born of *Male* and *Female* in the Spirit's realm in multitudes and individuations without number. And each of these primordial Beings is continuously active—within itself forever bringing forth—because its very being is defined by such engendering and bringing forth: as male and female energies, united in bipolar form.

What the primordial Human Being generates and manifests is, in effect, its very *self*—essence of its own eternal essence—albeit in more "compact," less translucent form. And, thus, continuing to manifest itself in forms increasingly more distant from its original creative source, the Human Being ultimately manifests itself in a specific spiritual "density," where it becomes discernible reality. And here it brings into existence, of its proper substance, all domains and worlds within creation, which equally reveal their essence as discernible reality.

Infinite in form and number is also the appearance, the discernible reality, of the eternal Human Being in its own self-revelation. And each succeeding self-reflection which it thus brings forth continues to bring forth the next, alike in kind, although of lower rank.

There are—not only in the spiritual, but even in the physically experienced cosmos—*human beings* of such awesome greatness that mortal man would rank them higher even than a god—if he were able to perceive them.

Among the lowest levels at which the human spirit manifests its nature is, however, that of mortal man on earth.

For in this mortal form, the Spirit-born eternal human has bound itself to one of the most narrowly restricted creatures of its own creation: the life form of the animal.

Born on earth into the body of an animal, the human spirit lost the consciousness of its true nature, its eternal self. It now is conscious of its being only through the cells of its material organism, whose specific rhythmic energies produce the self-awareness of the more developed human animal. Only those few rays of clouded light that still can reach the human spirit from its timeless home allow the mortal human's consciousness to rise above the level of its fellow creatures.

THE HUMAN BEING'S spirit would be doomed in animal embodiment if its divine inheritance, begotten of the Origin, had not been brought to earth behind it, so that the human spirit could once more be given the potential to receive within itself the Spirit's radiant crystal, formed of purest light, which then it will discover as its own, its *individuated* Living God.

Even as the builder of a well does not climb down into the deep without first having safely anchored the rope that is to raise him up again, so likewise did the human spirit not descend into the cosmos it created as perceptible reality, without providing safeguards to protect its issue: by virtue of the "silver cord" of radiant energies that link the human being to its primal generation in the Spirit.

Only due to this inborn connection can these energies, proceeding from the highest source, reach human beings even here on earth. And only these inherent energies enable human mortals to unify themselves with their eternal Living God and, strengthened thus, to make their long and much demanding way through night and darkness back into the realm of light.

Conscious of that powerful protection—once the Living God is "born" within the mortal's timeless soul—the human spirit then may fearlessly descend into the darkest vales through which its earthly fate might send it.

BUT AT THE PRESENT TIME most human souls still live within their mortal forms without their Living God, even though they worship an external godhead, an idol which they fashioned out of thoughts.

They also still expect to find the human being's ancient forebears only on this planet; for they are unaware that the entire universe is in effect the human being's realm. Nor do they realize that the surviving vestiges of "early man" which archeologists uncovered are only their *maternal*, earthly forebears, while their *paternal* ancestors, who are the spiritually informing element, can only be discovered in the Spirit's world.

It is not possible, however, to free the human spirit from its self-imposed confinement, which hinders it in mortal life, unless the human being finally begins to recognize that mortal man is only one among innumerable forms of human individuation. And thus one must abandon the presumptuous illusion that the mortal creature which inhabits this small planet represents the true, the one and only form of human life in all creation.

THE ANCIENT TEXTS of holy writ are the undoing of believers who assume that everything enlightened sages have entrusted to these books concerning "man" refers exclusively to mortal humans here on earth.

One's eyes must search for higher goals. Not, however, for a God enthroned above the clouds, but for the heights of one's own *self* in mankind's higher emanations. One must look upward to one's origin, the Spirit's radiant substance, which seeks to crystallize itself again within the human soul, and then becomes the human spirit's Living God.

But even finding their eternal Living God is difficult for mortals in this life; for they have grown accustomed to thinking of their fancied God as being only male, while in reality the human spirit's Living God embodies *male* and *female*.

In mortal life, the human spirit cannot find salvation from its bondage unless it will again grow conscious also of the *female* voice that speaks within its God.

"The Feminine Eternal attracts our souls to higher spheres."

Sensing but the *male* in one's imagined God is guilt; for this amounts to a rejection of the energies through which eternal Will gives life to *all* existence. It causes human mortals to fall victim to the passively conceiving impulse of their nature, and thus to sacrifice the active male component they possess.

Dissonance and conflict must of necessity ensue wherever in the cosmos the polarities of *male* and *female* are not joined in harmony.

To be sure, you here need not restrict yourself to using only terms like *male* and *female*.

Whatever words one uses, all life results from joining opposite polarities.

Positive and negative, active and passive; to beget and to bring forth, to give and to receive; to expel and to attract; to be the mover, or the object being moved.

And all this weaves itself into eternally recurring cycles, even as in life on earth the female grows to be the mother of the male, the male becomes the father of the female.

Nor is there in existence, either in the spiritual or in the physically experienced cosmos, any form or living thing, not even one ostensibly appearing to be "purely" male or female, in which the two polarities are not at work conjointly, although in countless variations.

Not one atom could escape disintegration into nothing, unless the energies of *male* and *female* were unceasingly creating and releasing power in its mass.

Whatever names one may assign to the minutest particles of matter which physical research is able to detect, the forces one is dealing with are always simply variant forms of the polarities of *male* and *female*, which have sustained all life from the Beginning.

Nor can you ever hope to find your Living God until you seek him in yourself: as *male* and *female* power; for only thus can God be truly found. And not until you sense him in this way will he be able to create himself in you: as that eternal *crystal*, wholly formed of purest light, uniting male and female, which then will unify the two polarities of your own nature within its own bipolar life.

If you will let these insights guide your inner quest, you shall be offered help from the eternal realm that is your spirit's home.

INVISIBLY ABIDING ON this planet lives an ancient One who is today as he has been in the Beginning—one who was begot and born as first the Spirit's *male* and *female* energies revealed themselves as Father and as Mother in the Origin—a Human Spirit of the highest order emanating from the radiant wellspring of eternal life in God.

One of those eternal emanations whom *Male* and *Female* in the Spirit first engender and bring forth "in their own image, after their own likeness."

There are, however, also other "human beings" present on this earth in unseen forms; beings who descend from those engendered in the Origin. As such, these stay "attached" to the creation they brought forth in the invisible domains of life, but nonetheless continue dwelling in the Spirit's worlds of light, because unlike the physically embodied human mortal, they had not "fallen" from that radiant life.

But knowing of the grievous plight of human spirits in their physical embodiment, they seek to rescue all that earnestly desire to be freed.

In offering their help, however, all of them are guided by the sublime Invisible, begotten of the Origin, who governs all things spiritual on earth.

This unseen hierarchy of helpers, guided by the highest Human Emanation in the Spirit, has been able, in each new generation, to find those mortals here on earth whom it could spiritually perfect to serve as instruments of its consuming will to help: as active *masters*, working from the highest form of spiritual knowledge found on earth. These few are able to take part in that eternal plan of rescue because they had already pledged themselves to serve that task *before* their incarnation in this earthly life.

These *masters* form the living "bridge" that has, throughout the ages, let the ancient Human of the Origin approach again his spiritual issue in its darkness—having fallen farthest from primeval light—enabling him to search for those whom he can raise and guide once more into the worlds of Light. But lacking that eternal "bridge" his help would not be possible.

THE REASON WHY SO FEW discover what so many seek is chiefly that most people continue searching in the wrong direction, and thus will lose themselves in ever darker crypts.

Every impulse seeks the goal toward which it is directed.

And thus it is that human mortals in whose life the *animal*, which gives their spirit earthly form, has gained the upper hand—causing them to take their creature life to be their true identity, indeed their very self—will search for, in the outer world, what they can only find within. For, in their inner life, the bridge to higher forms of human nature remains at all times open: owing to the *silver cord* of radiant energies, which link the human being's timeless essence, also that in mortal man, with all the Spirit's higher emanations.

It follows that no helper from the Spirit's realm, nor any of the *masters*—who embody final knowledge here on earth in mortal form to serve the Human of the Origin as spiritual bridges—can ever reach the human mortal's inmost self-awareness except from deep within; for only there can one discover all things human in the highest sense.

Although a mortal's human essence can also be "inspired" from without—from the invisible dimension of material nature—this only can prepare that latent essence, so that it may be guided and enlightened from within, once it has indeed awakened.

If those who seek would truly find, they need to aim their efforts toward their inner life.

Neither in Tibetan monasteries, nor at the holy shrines of India, and not in any esoteric circles of presumed "initiates" does one attain the *great enlightenment*—the state of final Buddhahood—but only in profoundest inner solitude: alone with the eternal *human* essence abiding in one's heart.

Among the very few on earth who were perfected to be *masters* that embody final knowledge, in order to bring help to their afflicted fellow mortals, there is not one who could approach your real self—even if he stood in front of you in person—unless your self-awareness has awakened in that inner realm in which alone your consciousness can comprehend your human essence.

N ow, to continue, let me speak to you as to a reader who absorbed with a receptive mind what I have so far had to tell you.

I take it, then, you are resolved to reach, within yourself, the human being's higher forms: by virtue of the timeless human essence that lies hidden in your own immortal nature?

In other words, you are determined to retrace your path to your eternal origin within the Spirit, patiently ascending step by step?

You did not merely read my words the way one listens to a fairy tale, but earnestly intend to follow my advice with all your strength and will?

Be mindful, then, of what I further have to tell you.

As i already pointed out above, the spiritually engendered Human Being—begot and born of *Male* and *Female* in the Spirit—is by nature likewise *male* and *female*.

Throughout the Spirit's realm, the human being, from the highest level to the lowest, down to mortal man on earth, will always be encountered as both *male* and *female*. And only in this unified polarity shall also you find human beings in the Spirit's realm, as soon as you yourself are found within that world: as someone who is capable of finding.

At that time, a *master*, one endowed with final knowledge, will be sent you from the Spirit's realm to be your inner guide and helper. Who it is, you do not know, nor can your eyes perceive him. Only through a new kind of awareness can you feel that he is present. That inner helper, too, is *male* and *female* unified; for that which reaches you through him—and cannot reach you any other way—is truly the eternal Human of the Spirit, who has arisen from its sepulcher, in him, the human mortal.

If you seek the Spirit's light, remember that your path shall be protected by the Masters serving the eternal Day, whose dawn shall vanquish all the darkness that surrounds you.

You also need to know, however, who these *masters* are, and where you ought to seek them; for that which has its life in them, and wants to bring you help, is not encountered in your outer world, nor conquered by external means.

It is not their bodily appearance in the world your senses can perceive that makes them capable of bringing you the help you need.

You must not look for them in this external world, beclouded by unknowing, where the sophisticated mortal creature, which here provides the human spirit with a body as a needed tool, is given to deceive itself in its own way, mistaking semblance for reality, much beset by doubts and ever subject to despair.

Within that outer world you have been searching all your life, yet never found what you had sought.

You now must aim your searches at a different realm; a world that you have overlooked until this day.

Never during life on earth in mortal form can you experience final clarity concerning who and what you truly are, before you shall have found the human being—begotten in the Origin—within your own eternal self.

You cannot find that human being, however, except by climbing, step by step, the Spirit's "Jacob's ladder," whose lowest rungs, which touch the earth, are human mortals. Yet in these mortals the Human Being's highest emanation is already lord and king.

Your search for final truth in "sacred" books of ancient times will benefit you little, because these texts were written in their day for only those who long had found such final truth, and were to serve them merely as companions on their journey through this life.

In such books, a master speaks to a disciple with whom his spirit is already one, so that he can reveal himself in images and symbols the pupil knows and understands.

Once having found within you—in your eternal human nature—what now you merely seek, many ancient texts will speak to you as well in clear, intelligible language. Only then will these time-honored "sacred books" prove useful also to your own pursuit.

For now, however, you should only seek within yourself.

ABOVE ALL ELSE YOU MUST begin by calling forth, whenever you say "I," no longer just the sublimated creature aspect of your nature, but your eternal *human* self.

It is *male* and *female* you must seek—in all things that abide within you and above you.

Whether you are male or female, always bear in mind that you alone determined your polarity, from the Beginning, and that this polar self-expression cannot change again through all eternity, but that, within itself, it always wants its needed opposite.

The male component of your nature must not suppress your female side, nor must your female side negate your nature's male component.

Only thus shall you one day be reunited, also in the Spirit's world, with your eternal polar opposite. And both polarities shall then be unified in one, even as they were before their separation had become inevitable, owing to the "fall" from light into the world of matter.

Pursue your quest the proper way, as I advise you in this book, and you shall one day find your own self as a human being of the Spirit.

In that eternal human being—within your own enduring self—you then shall step by step ascend, united with your Living God, and once again return to your beginning—the first-engendered state from which your consciousness was severed by an act of your own will—

begot and born within the Spirit, eternally alive within the Spirit's world: sustained by Male and Female.

NOT EVERYONE IS ABLE to awaken in the highest world of spiritual reality already during life on earth, while still in animal embodiment.

In this physical existence only very few experience fully lucid consciousness within the spiritual dimension of this earth.

But all are capable of finding—already here and in their days on earth—their own eternal life within.

ALL, WITHOUT EXCEPTION, must one day learn to find that inner life, even if they had not found it by the time they shall have to depart this earthly life.

You cannot find yourself alive and fully conscious in the radiant worlds of Spirit, unless you first have found that Spirit's life within yourself.

Not until you live your own eternal life can you experience your own essence as a human self whose presence is eternity.

And, thus, the radiant Master's hallowed counsel also speaks to you:

"Be perfect, then, even as your Father in heaven is perfect."

Yet not your earthly attributes and nature can ever rise to the "perfection" that he meant.

Only when you shall have found your own eternal life within, and truly live that inner life, shall you be "perfect" like the "Father," who abides in "heaven": eternal Procreator in the Ground of all Becoming—primal Energy embracing primal *Being*—*Male* at once and *Female*.

Before you have achieved what here you truly can accomplish you should not let one day pass by that did not see you make at least an effort striving for so high a goal.

CHAPTER TWO

THE PATH
OF THE FEMALE

WITHIN THE HIGHEST sphere of worlds made manifest as spiritual reality, wherein the Spirit's human essence for the first time generates itself as manifest appearance—which here is still of purely spiritual substance—the elements of Male and Female continue to be closely joined in their originally given unity of self-experience in bipolar form.

The spiritual worlds, however, in which this primal human emanation of the Spirit continues to engender its own self grow ever "denser," as it were, with each successive generation, reflecting less and less of their originally given Light. Nonetheless, in all these worlds the male and female elements remain connected in the closest union of their joint bipolar self-experience.

Having finally arrived in this descent at its most compact, "densest" state of spiritual form—here illuminated only dimly by the radiance it had possessed in the Beginning—the human spirit that is occupying these dimensions, whose nature is so very far removed from the domain of its primordial generation, now for the first time comes to know the outer worlds of physical creation.

At this very threshold, however, a new sensation overwhelms the human spirit's female pole: the consciousness of fear.

As a unified, bipolar being, the human spirit had until this time been able to subdue and dominate the awesome forces which it now, however, sees at work in ways so new and alien to its own existence that here it dares no longer to assert its will and, consequently, loses its inherent power.

Yet at work behind the forces which it now envisions as a threat, the human spirit grows aware of the existence of a new and different world; a world containing living creatures, all engendered by its own inherent powers at the Spirit's highest plane: the world of physically perceived reality, where spiritual beings experience their own presence in material form.

Fear of the chaotic elements over which it now has lost control, combined with the attraction exerted by the forms perceived as physical reality, ultimately cause the human spirit's female pole to breach—by force of will—the parting wall which until then had stood between itself and the dimension of the physically experienced universe.

Driven by the knowledge of this newly found domain of unimagined forms of self-experience, its total being trembling with desire, the female pole now separates itself from what had been its given state of being, determined to unite itself with a material form—the body of an animal—much like a bolt of lightning flashes from a cloud, wanting to be married to the earth.

Throughout the limitless expanse of the material universe there are innumerable planets on which the human spirit now is forced to undergo such self-experience in an animal body, as a creature in material form. Traces of that animal are still preserved on earth from ages when it was not yet the vessel of the human spirit, even though such remnants are today regarded as evidence of "early man."

With its willful separation from the worlds of spiritual perception, together with the newly sought attachment to a creature body of material form, the human spirit's "Fall" from highest Light has been irrevocably consummated.

As a result, the human spirit, which until now had been both male and female—united in unseparated consciousness, continuously manifesting its existence in successive spiritual dimensions—is now effectively divided. For, in the world of matter, the polar opposites of male and female must be severed, of necessity, because this world exists by virtue of the "tension" generated by the separation of the poles, which had themselves been formed in the Beginning.

It is the female pole within the human being's spiritual nature who in effect initiates the "Fall," who ardently desires life in physical embodiment. But given that, in spiritual dimensions, no being can exist in which a single male or female pole is active by itself, the male polarity must needs accompany its partner in the "Fall."

The specific animal body which the female pole at once discovers in its "Fall"—a form long since "created" by human spirits of the earliest generation—now becomes the body which the male polarity must correspondingly desire also for itself.

"But when the sons of the Gods beheld that the daughters of earth were fair, they chose them as their wives."

(At this point, the former "daughters of the Gods" already had become the "daughters of the earth." The "sons of the Gods" now follow after them.)

IN THIS WAY ONE MAY attempt, in earthly terms, to picture the eternally recurring process that finally subjects the human being, an emanation generated in the Spirit's realm, to bondage in this world of matter, the realm of physical perception.

What here occurs is fundamentally a change from one form of perception to another. It is a change initiated by the female pole, which instantly divides the formerly combined polarities into separately existing male and female beings, corresponding to the gender separation of the human mortal creature, which can exist in only this divided state.

In the story of the Garden of Eden, it is the "serpent" who entices "Eve," who then seduces "Adam." Although this myth, as known today, may not have been transmitted in its original form, it still shows clearly that its author spoke with knowledge of an eternally recurring spiritual event and wanted to convey his insight, veiled in the symbolic language of his time, to later generations, provided they could understand the meaning of his allegory.

Knowing how to read the imagery of this enlightened witness, one readily will also find the consequences of the "Fall" for man and woman, in their divided state, distinguished very clearly in the words he has the Lord address to "Adam" and "Eve." For here he measures the degree of culpability, and the ensuing burdens, by drawing a significant distinction.

In the consummation of this endlessly occurring "Fall" it is, in each and every instance, the human spirit's female pole—whose given power is a passive force—which generates the "primal guilt" by giving way to fear. For in this way it first succumbs to the magnetic energy exerted by the worlds of physical creation.

Even so, the human spirit's male polarity is not by any means exempt from guilt, as if it merely were the hapless "victim" of its union with a female counterpart.

The guilt that weighs upon the male polarity results from the surrender of its active role, its failure to resist when, during life in its bipolar state, its female pole sustained the threat of fear and powerful attraction.

And thus it comes about that both polarities effectively reverse their given roles—the female pole becoming active, the male becoming passive—amounting to a spiritual perversion, which makes the human spirit's "Fall" into the worlds of physical perception unavoidable.

The decisive factor counting here as spiritual "guilt," however, remains explicitly the concrete act of will committed by the human spirit's female pole.

Hence the "curse" which, in the myth that tells about the "fall of man," is laid upon humanity, exemplified in mortal woman, foretelling her the pains, distress, and labor that her earthly life cannot be spared, as well as the persistent struggle against the lure of the beguiling "serpent," the experience of reality through physical perception.

The curse imposed upon the male polarity, by contrast, only causes physical perception in itself to lose its given value.

The burdens laid on him consist of only the relentless toil and sweat to which this earthly form of life remains so closely chained.

Therefore, as the myth continues, the Lord enjoins the human spirit's female pole, "You are to be your husband's subject, and he is to rule over you."

How often has this word not been abused: as willful license to suppress a woman's indi-

THE PATH OF THE FEMALE

viduality, when it was made the spurious pre-
text justifying absolute dominion of the male
in marriage!

Yet all the condescending or disdainful scorn
this passage may arouse cannot invalidate the
weighty truth the ancient sage had stated
through the mouth of "God"; for only as divine
commands addressed to man and woman did
he judge these words to have sufficient
emphasis.

The meaning of this passage is very different
from what is sought in it by those who would
derive from this all but transparent revelation simply an expedient, divinely sanctioned
affirmation to justify the claims that untamed
male ambition makes to absolute dominion
over woman.

Instead, this counsel shows unto the physically divided poles how they shall one day be
united once again within the Spirit's world.
For only through *reversing* the spiritual perversion of the poles, which had produced the
"Fall," can this reunion be achieved.

These words lay stress upon the spiritual law
that will let only male polarities assist it here

on earth, when it has need of mortals as "antennas," in order to transmit anew the "joyous tidings" sent forth by the Spirit's highest human emanation. For thus it seeks to make that message once again accessible to those who stumble without guidance through the dark of earthly life, and to convey to them the energies they need on their return into the realm of Light.

Even in this physically restricted world both man and woman still retain the last few traces of their life as one bipolar entity in ages past.

In woman, here on earth, there still survives a kind of "memory" that she had long ago, in spiritual life, experienced her own being also in a man, within a male polarity; even as the man in mortal life is able to detect, within himself, the same surviving traces of his formerly bipolar life, united with a woman.

All inner striving for emotional unity, for harmony between both man and woman in this life is ultimately rooted only in such recollection of what the woman's soul still knows of man, and what the soul of man still knows of woman.

Nor could even the tremendous force of sexual attraction between some persons of both genders manifest itself—a power vested in the human being's animal existence—if any opposition, potentially existing in a person's soul, had not been practically eliminated by virtue of a distant "memory," preserved within that soul, as one last "recollection" of its polar integration long ago.

No kind of inner "understanding" touching man and woman would be possible in physical embodiment, were it not for the effects that still assert themselves in woman from her former union with a male polarity, or those still active in a man from his long since abandoned female counterpart.

Not all the spirit's human individuations have been victims of the "Fall" and thus compelled to undergo the separation of their polar unity.

Those who had not known the "Fall" nor the ensuing separation, and who abide within the spiritual dimension of the earth, are the continuously self-renewing source of a consuming, love-inspired will to help; a will whose only goal and purpose is to reach those human

spirits who had fallen into the domain of physically experienced life, and from this state to
lead them back again into the light of their
eternal origin.

These still united human emanations, abiding in the Spirit, are the powers—and it is they
alone—who, here on earth, discover those
awakened souls who, long before their birth,
had pledged themselves as helpers in their
work. These helpers, then, are raised by them
to the perfection of transcendent knowing that
all active Masters must possess.

The unified eternal individuations unerringly
discover and select, in every generation, those
human males in whom they recognize the spiritual individuality that long ago had of its own
free will resolved to serve them; men who thus
are able to become their spiritual "sons" and
"brothers," and whom they now will make their
Mediators, as Luminaries of eternal Light.

These invisible bipolar human powers dwell,
as I have said above, within the spiritual
dimension of this earth, where they are guided by the boundless love and mercy of one
of those sublimest human emanations of the

Origin, who will eternally remain within the Spirit's innermost dimensions and do not want to manifest their issue even in domains of spiritual reality.

In accordance with eternal spiritual law, it is exclusively the human spirit's male component which, although embodied here in creature form, continues to possess the faculty permitting it to enter, and consciously to apprehend, the spiritual dimension of the earth; the sphere in which abide the undivided emanations of the Spirit, as helpers of humanity.

It follows, then, that woman here on earth, the mortal form embodying the human spirit's female pole, could never be transformed into a Master of eternal Light. Nor could a real Master accept a woman as his spiritually adopted "son," or make of her a true initiate; for all these forms of active spiritual energy, which are distinct as such and independent of capricious whim, inevitably presuppose the human mortal's male polarity.

Woman, here on earth, who is the human spirit's separated, passive, female pole, must now confront the consequences in her mortal life of having willed the impulse toward embodiment in earthly form, which unavoidably imposed the separation of the male and female poles.

To be sure, the human spirit's physically embodied female pole can certainly be "lifted up" into the spiritual dimension of the earth, even during mortal life, but only in a passive manner, consistent with a woman's nature, and without gaining final consciousness in that domain. However, this does not in any way preclude a woman from receiving, through influence of male polarities, spiritual insights and direction.

The incarnation of the human spirit's male polarity, by contrast, continues to possess its active spiritual energy, even in man's earthly form. Yet this potential, latent power can in practice be awakened, either wholly or in part, only in a few exceptional cases, which I already have discussed.

This awakening can only be effected by the liberating help of those who live in undivided form within the planet's spiritual dimension. And in their sphere the spirit's male polarity will then be consciously alive and active, either in complete lucidity, or in at least a partially receptive state.

But even though the human spirit's active male polarity may have been fully, partially, or intermittently awakened by the mentioned helpers, it could not consciously exist in their exalted realm without a complementing female pole. Consequently, there descends a ray of female polar nature from the heights of unformed, all-embracing Spirit—from the Light of the Beginning, embracing male and female—which unifies its substance with that individuated human spirit and thus endows it with the requisite perfection.

The poet doubtless was aware of these events when intuition gifted him to write, "The Feminine Eternal attracts our souls to higher spheres."

The Male Eternal, on the other hand, can doubtless raise the human being's female pole into the light of spiritual dimensions, even though it is not possible to have that pole gain consciousness in these domains while it is still embodied in this present life.

It was an act of will—the striving toward the world perceived through physical, material senses—and the consequent reversal of its spiritually given passive nature into purely active power which caused the human spirit's female pole to forfeit, of its own volition, the very energy that might have gained it freedom from the bondage to this life of physical perception, whose nature it had once desired to possess.

The spiritual energy disabled by this act of will is not to be restored again in mortal life on earth.

Even so, the masters of eternal Light—who serve the undivided human emanations in the planet's spiritual dimension as a living "bridge"—would free both man and woman from the yoke they bear in creature life.

This they can accomplish, if first they have been able to motivate the will of either man or woman to unify their soul's dynamic elements with their eternal spiritual self.

Then only can the human spirit's Living God be "born" again within that mortal's soul.

And only then shall once again be "set up on the earth" the timeless "Jacob's ladder" on which the "angels" are beheld "ascending and descending"; the ladder that is reaching from this world "to heaven," into the Light of the Beginning, which is the final source of every mortal human's spiritual nature.

THE INNER PATHS that I describe are barred to neither man nor woman.

Beyond these paths, however, I also speak of a particular ascent, which must at times be undertaken by a man, but never by a woman.

I speak of the ability to enter the spiritual dimension of the earth—and consciously to act within that plane, even during mortal life— as a potential faculty that may be found in men, even though in practice such men are very few.

A woman—and that pertains to every woman who, knowingly or trusting intuition, follows paths like those that I describe—will gain the power to raise herself to conscious life within the worlds of Spirit only after the completion of a well-directed life. And she will then be gifted with that power through a Master, one of those whom the Eternal Feminine already had "attracted," during their external life, onto the spiritual dimension of the earth, and who continue helping human spirits from that sphere, where they abide, close to this earth, even after having left their mortal forms.

The lofty path of woman—although not limited to woman only—is thus an indirect ascent. Yet, in the end, that path will lead the human spirit to the same perfection as the male's direct approach, which very few are able to pursue; namely, to the spiritual integration of the male and female poles, and thus to fully conscious individuation. And this will come about in spheres of spiritual reality that lie at infinitely higher planes than just the "life beyond," wherein each human spirit finds itself at death—even without effort—as soon as it has lost its mortal body, and thus awakens on the "other side," the world external senses cannot apprehend.

Still, a woman here on earth would seek in vain to find a Master of eternal Light in this existence hoping that he might effect her entry into spheres of spiritual perception while she was still alive in mortal form.

Not even those most venerable women who used to serve the Master whom the Gospel texts proclaim had found in him the helper who was able to unlock for them the Spirit's inner realms before their earthly life had been fulfilled, and he himself delivered of his earthly form.

Before that time they did not "recognize" him as the one he was, but took him for a "gardener" tending earthly grounds.

It was a harsh rebuke with which this Master of eternal Light had once rejected even his own mother, saying, "Woman, what have I to do with you?"

Yet with these words he speaks for the external, physical appearance of every spiritually integrated Master. And what he says relates to every woman who on earth, and in her temporal appearance, seeks to find the special help that one of those whose work affects the Spirit's realm can grant her only after he himself has laid his mortal form to rest.

"But once I have been lifted up from the earth, I shall draw all things toward me."

DEEPLY ROOTED EARTHLY longings all too often caused the souls of women searching for their master to pursue mistaken paths; paths on which delusions, generated by a psychic split of consciousness, would let them find the fancied "master," who was nothing other than a phantom of inflamed imagination.

Mortal woman far too often has in truth been seeking mortal man, even though her ardent faith made her believe she was ascending toward a counterpart within the realm of Spirit, be it in the form of "Krishna" or of "Jesus."

Whether in such worship then the "bridegroom of the soul" will be embraced with fiery faith, or, burning with compassion, life and suffering of the "beloved" are experienced in ecstatic bliss—the vision is, in every case, a psychic phantom, triggered by a split of personality. No matter how sublime and moving the signs of such disorders may appear, or how dramatically the apparition even may affect the victim's mortal body. Often such emotional tumult will furthermore attract the denizens of nature's hidden realm; creatures one would flee from in sheer horror if their nature and effects were understood.

WHEN MORTAL WOMAN shall be free again of the material body she had once desired, having lived a life devoted to the goal of one day gaining back her conscious self within the Spirit, in timeless form and with a soul uniting every element, illuminated by her Living God—only then can she expect a Master to approach her in his timeless form and thus restore to her what long ago she had to leave behind where—as the human being's female pole—her power had been paralyzed by the inversion of her will.

And then she also will be certain to find the spiritual counterpart again with whom she once had been united, and henceforth shall exist as one for all eternity: a "perfect" human being in the Spirit, conscious of her own self in that integrated individuation and—at the same time and within that selfsame individuation—also conscious of her spirit's male identity.

But all of this is true as well of every male in mortal life. The sole exceptions being those few that are born with the capacity to be perfected and to work as Masters of transcendent knowing. And this capacity is the result of their specific "spiritual heritage": the age-old elements that unified themselves within their souls, in consequence of their commitment, made already in the Spirit's realm, to serve the Luminaries of eternal Light as active helpers here on earth. Excepted, too, are those who have at least sufficiently awakened during mortal life, so that a Master can adopt them as "spiritual sons," and thus endow them with the faculty of conscious self-experience in the world of Spirit.

Yet even one who has been born to be a Master, or one who was adopted as a Master's spiritual "son," can make effective use of his inherent spiritual potential only if he will at all times faithfully, and with courageous resolution, follow the directions given him by those who are his inner guides.

The spiritual hierarchy brooks neither arbitrary choices nor capricious will.

Every man and every woman embodied here on earth in mortal form at all times occupy the very place they have been able to attain; and none is ever given more than what his own endeavor prepared him to receive.

YET IF I HERE WOULD show the female's path into the Spirit, I still must mention that, for woman in her mortal form, there is a special difference in following this path, even on that part of the ascent which is identical for man and woman.

The male who sets out on this path is certain to attain his goal more quickly if he pursues it with an active attitude, at all times "reaching," as it were, for the desired goal.

A woman, on the other hand, will reach her goal more easily if she pursues her quest through faith; by trusting in a state of mind that strives to reach its goal, though not by means of "grasping" it, but rather by allowing to be led to its attainment in a passive way.

This insight rests on ancient practical experience, and if it is correctly understood it can prove very helpful to both man and woman in pursuing their respective goals.

The path of woman, like the path of man, is a return to the original condition in which the human being used to live within the Spirit's world—before imprisoning its spiritual senses in the animal's material organism, thus making them incapable of any longer apprehending timeless life.

By reversing what had been its spiritually anchored passive nature, and turning it into an active force, the human spirit's female pole had brought about its own paralysis, and thus deprived itself of its originally given power.

If in time to come that power is to be re-gained, it is essential that one voluntarily adopt again the polar orientation of one's own beginning.

ALIKE IN MORTAL WOMAN as in man the Living God desires to be "born"—already here and now—while they still live their life on earth.

The "inner journey" I described in its specific stages in the first work of this trilogy, *The Book on the Living God*, is a path prepared for every human being here on earth, be it man or woman. And everything I stated there concerning spiritual guidance, the voice and nature of the inner guide, and the effective help received from those who are the Masters active in the Spirit, all that is equally accessible to man as well as woman.

Let no reader be deceived and think that in my books I merely wish to write about the possibilities for spiritual development that none but rare exceptions can pursue; such as the path of an initiate, a Master's "son" or pupil, let alone the one that only Masters of eternal Light are able to ascend.

Everything I say about such special paths, in each case pointing at them only from afar, consistent with my obligation, is, without exception, presented in a way that no one can be left in doubt.

I more than once have pointed out that these most arduous paths are not accessible to many, but yield themselves to only those few men who have been born to scale them.

Now in the present chapter I had to touch on many things pertaining equally to man and woman; for otherwise I could not have so clearly shown the difference between the normal path of woman, and the particular ascent that only men can undertake who have been born as Mediators of eternal Light, or those intended to become their pupils.

Even though the path of woman may not attain that final peak in life on earth which only those are able to ascend who have been born to work as Masters holding final knowledge, the woman's path shall reach the same goal in the end: fully conscious self-awareness in the worlds of spiritual existence, culminating in the rebirth of the human being in eternal spiritual form—the union of the male and female in abiding joy, in one eternally inseparable self, experienced as bipolar being.

Any goal the male is able to attain within the Spirit shall one day also be attainable again to woman, by virtue of the male.

It then shall be the human being's male polarity that draws the female pole aloft, much as the female pole had once impelled the male polarity to follow its descent into the realm of physical perception.

CHAPTER THREE

THE PATH
OF THE MALE

IN VIEW OF WHAT I HAD to say in describing "The Path of the Female," it well might seem superfluous to devote a special chapter also to "The Path of the Male."

In the majority of cases, the path will not be markedly different for either man or woman, despite their clear distinctiveness as spiritual polarities. Only in the way of following that path the male's approach can differ from the course pursued by woman.

There is but one part on that path restricted to the male polarity as such and, therefore, not accessible to woman during physical embodiment. And that most toilsome part of the ascent is barred to all but those few men who have been born here for the purpose of attaining the potential of fully conscious active life within the Spirit's world already in their mortal days.

In any case, that final stretch of the ascent is of a kind that no one—neither man nor woman—would ever want to follow them, even if they could in mortal life.

It would display the height of witless arrogance if any male on earth assumed that he was spiritually "privileged" simply for being a "man," and consequently deemed a woman's spiritual potential of lower value than his own.

I purposely lay stress on "spiritual potential"; for I am speaking of realities effective in the Spirit, not merely properties of intellect, nor the capacity for abstract speculation, which are no more than products of development through physical conditioning.

Within the worlds of Spirit there is no difference in worth or rank between the male and female individuations.

The passive nature of the female, together with the active nature of the male have been implanted in the Spirit's human being from the Origin, in equal might and power.

The few exceptional males who, during life on earth, might rightly claim a spiritual "prerogative"—not granted to the human spirit's female pole in physical embodiment—have always been aware of their explicit obligation to offer mortal woman their especial help; for as the primal impulse toward embodiment in earthly life had first arisen in the female pole, the latter faces a more difficult condition owing to the "Fall" than does the human male.

None among them has at any time thought less of woman than of man, let alone regarded mortal woman with disdain.

Despite the fact that one of them spoke harshly when he felt it necessary to draw a clear distinction between his *temporal* relation to a mortal woman here on earth and his eternal *spiritual* identity, all who truly were entitled to that spiritual preference—applying both to men and women—have given proof of their profound respect for woman, also in her physical embodiment.

Nor should that be surprising, given that in each of those who have attained perfection there is present, from the moment of their having reached that state, no longer just the human spirit's *male* polarity, but unified with it—in substitution of the *female* pole, with which he one day shall be reunited—the needed ray of female spiritual polarity from the eternal Light of the Beginning—the "Feminine Eternal"—through which alone the human male polarity grows capable of gaining fully conscious life within the Spirit, the worlds that manifest themselves as *spiritual* reality.

How, indeed, could a perfected being of that kind—even if in life on earth appearing only as the human spirit's male embodiment—ever deem the female spirit to be in any way inferior to the male? The very spirit which, within his timeless essence, his male polarity perceives as one within its own eternal self?

"THE PATH OF THE MALE" demands of him who would pursue it, from the outset, both an earnest, but also a well-practiced will to understand a woman's point of view.

A man in whom such willingness is lacking shall never reach the goal he otherwise might have attained.

A woman, if she has reclaimed her passive orientation, tends to be far more inclined to recognize and willingly accept the male's inherent nature, not seldom even with respect.

The active nature of the male, by contrast, all too often will subject a man to the delusion of his inherent "superiority," so that he feels entitled not to see in woman a different self of equal worth, but something he believes inferior.

This in fact presents a fairly serious obstacle for not a few who otherwise are quite prepared and willing to pursue the path of the male.

There will be some who feel convinced of being on their way; indeed, who see themselves quite thoroughly inspirited, and thus presume that they are justified in looking down on woman from the heights of their imagined superiority. Yet in this way they only forfeit every possibility of ever apprehending spiritual life.

But any man who sensed that even from the first, as he is taking his initial steps upon his inner path, his being is "attracted" by the Feminine Eternal—whose power flows from highest spiritual hierarchies down to their appointed helpers, who live on earth in mortal form to reach and to direct him—that man will hardly deem himself "superior" to woman, simply for being male.

He, instead, will render unto woman the things that are a woman's, and unto man the things that are a man's; knowing clearly that the human being dwelling in the Spirit's realm can only come to life again in its eternal, absolute perfection if male and female energies shall one day reunite themselves once more to form a single spiritual entity, within whose consciousness he then discovers both himself and his eternal counterpart, integrated in a single timeless self.

In India, this event was represented even in most ancient times by images of lingam and of yoni in conjunction. The emblem of lingam, or phallus, by itself, however, as the correlative material organ of the human male, symbolically expressed the given energy whose nature generates, in men selected to that end from birth, the true initiate and the authentic Master of eternal Light.

Even the practice of immolating widows, found in ancient India, which had its origins in the religiously oriented will of the surviving spouse, must be viewed as only the pathetic vestige of a spiritual truth received through a tradition going back to still much earlier times. But since its meaning was no longer understood, that truth became corrupted and was given a distorted form.

One carried to extremes, in this external life, what ought to have been comprehended as a symbol, in purely spiritual terms. But it has always been the fate of every truth revealed on earth that it can brightly shine for but a little while, and will be grasped by only few, before it is made "common knowledge" and obscured by all too earthly misconceptions.

IF "WOMAN" WOULD GROW whole again through "man," and "man" grow whole through "woman," then both of them must seek to find the way ascending to the Spirit in mutual understanding, their souls united in a single will, even as they once had lost their presence in the Spirit's life conjointly, when they were one in their resolve.

One will hardly doubt that through such inner unity in striving for a common spiritual goal some rays of light must also fall on problems of external life; problems that, before such joint resolve, had truly been a serious burden to both partners, and well might have appeared unsolvable.

Having one day reached the goal that all are able to attain on earth who truly are determined to achieve it—their hearts enlightened by their Living God—both man and woman will at last be swept aloft by powers from on high; powers that at all times flow through those few mortal Mediators who serve Divine Love as its guides, to lead back onto higher planes all such who long for Light, and for deliverance from the chaotic night of will devoid of purpose.

More effectively than all instruction through the spoken or the written word could ever hope to do, all earnest seekers after truth are safely guided from those worlds of radiant light which only Masters having knowledge of eternal life are able to experience; for they alone are capable, already during life in mortal form, knowingly to enter and be active in these realms, being fully conscious of their timeless individuality.

One day free again from earthly bondage, man and woman shall be joined once more within a single conscious self, while perfectly retaining their respective individuations—indeed their given polar natures as two distinctive spiritual beings. For, in that newborn spiritual identity, their separate "selves" shall then completely coincide, so that each independent "self" will apprehend the "self" within its counterpart as if it were its own.

What had been Two in separation shall then become united in a Third as One: a newly integrated spiritual individuation comprising man and woman, inseparably joined for all eternity.

To make it possible for every man and every woman to receive such help and guidance, so that, after having lived their days on earth, they can accomplish this reunion; to show them how this earthly life may be transformed into a blessing, how waste of energy and fruitless byways are avoided—those are the tasks for which the Masters of Compassion, whose knowledge searches final things, are born as mortals into life on earth.

It is not what they may possess in terms of intellect and mental powers that makes them competent to help and guide their fellow mortals.

Neither special "talents" nor acquired "learning" have made them what they are.

Farsightedness in earthly matters is not what gives them final insight into life in the dimensions of the Spirit.

All their "knowing" flows from Love that inwardly illuminates its object.

All their "knowledge" rests on certainty that only Truth within the Spirit can impart.

They alone are able to ascend that final summit crowning the path of the male, where they attain the power consciously to function and perform their tasks within the Spirit's world, the world whose very substance is self-conscious Light. And only from that inmost realm flows all the help that, through the Luminaries, who mediate eternal Light, becomes accessible to mortals.

CHAPTER FOUR

MARRIAGE

SEXUAL COMPANIONSHIP uniting man and woman in this present life is one thing; a very different thing, however, is true marriage.

Anyone who grasped the essence of the mystery surrounding male and female, a mystery ascending to the inmost realms of Spirit—indeed, unto the Light of the Beginning—will look upon monogamy as sacred, as a bond between one woman and one man that is to last while both shall live on earth.

Blest are those who, in this present life, are married to their timeless spiritual counterpart: the other self with whom they one day shall be reunited to form a single individuation in the Spirit, given they had long ago been *one*, before their separation owing to the "Fall."

Some may well enjoy this blessing without suspecting their good luck. But it will always be a case of special "luck," because the paths the separated spirits follow are not so parallel in their direction that such reunions could too often come about in life on earth.

In the majority of marriages, the poles that found each other in this present life will not be those that once had been united in the same eternal being.

Yet once they have been joined together, of their own free will, to share this present life, both partners are accountable to cosmic law, and thus are obligated to regard their bond as if, eternities ago, they had in fact existed as a single spiritual being and now were once again united, to live their life as one inseparable human spirit for all time to come.

Here on earth, only those whose spiritual senses have entirely awakened can ever know with certainty whether their companion in this present life is truly their eternal counterpart or not.

In the perplexing labyrinth of earthly life, deceptions beckon at each turn.

Some will regard themselves as "reunited" spirits, such as I here described it, although they will not be in fact; while others might be tempted, owing to the physically acquired differences in their mental and emotional life, to think that they are strangers, yet will indeed be counterparts that once had formed the same eternal being in the Spirit, before their separation.

Not having yet awakened in the Spirit's life to lucid self-awareness, who would here presume to venture final judgment?

Highest cosmic law therefore demands that all who choose their partner of their own free will resolve to act as if they both were certain that they had once existed as a single spiritual self, and one day shall again be reunited in the Spirit's world to live that undivided life through all eternity.

Reprehensible is any compact joining man and woman if they are not determined to live according to this charge.

"What you have done to the least of my brothers, you have done it unto me,"—that is how the Master whom the Gospel texts proclaim had once advised his pupils.

But in the same way it is true to say, "Whatever you shall do to the respective male or female counterpart with whom you share your married life on earth, you shall have done that to *yourself*; but also, most assuredly, to your own eternal counterpart, whether you in truth have found your being's other half already in this present life—or not.

It is your *own* eternal self that you are forming in the life you share in marriage here on earth. And the more closely you approach perfection in forming your potential— according to the high demands of your eternal life as a bipolar spiritual being, destined to be joined again in union—the sooner, too, shall you one day be able to exchange the restless way of life in separation for the timeless undivided state that once again restores in you your nature's other pole, in whom you then shall also find *yourself*.

Of all the efforts, patience, all the self-restraint your marriage may demand of you, not one iota will be lost; for everything you make your own by virtue of self-discipline will then be yours forever.

In every sphere of life on earth, each human being can, at times, become the agent acting for another.

Your conduct toward your fellow mortals will of necessity produce its consequences; and those consequences will reflect the nature of your deeds.

If you have ever done an evil thing to anyone, neither watchfulness nor cunning can protect you from having to experience evil of the self-same kind. And here it does not matter whether retribution finds you through the person you had harmed, or whether someone else is acting in his place. Nor does it matter whether you will suffer evil of the sort that you committed, or whether it returns to you in other forms.

In every instance will it correspond exactly to the measure of affliction you had caused.

The person bringing ill upon you is only acting for the one that you had harmed; even if the victim of your deed has long ago wholeheartedly forgiven you and would by nature be incapable of ever seeking personal revenge.

You well may find *forgiveness*, but you will not escape your *karma*—the accumulated consequences of your deeds.

Perhaps you feel your triumph is assured because those consequences did not show their face at once—however, do not celebrate too soon!

Although it might take many years, the day will surely come when you yourself shall have to suffer what you have done to others.

And if the proper time to balance your account does not present itself while you still live on earth, you nonetheless shall in the same way have to settle what you owe in other forms of life—for in these matters there is no escape.

What here is said concerning evil things that you have done to others is true no less of all things good; indeed, of even the most hidden act of kindness through which you brought some joy into a fellow human's life.

The consequences of your actions cannot be undone; nor is there any need for you to know whoever shall one day be acting as their agent.

Sooner or later will that person come into your life, unawares that through his actions—be they good or ill—he simply functions as the tool that executes the consequences you yourself created by your deeds.

AND IN THE SAME WAY will you foster consequences for yourself by virtue of your conduct toward your counterpart on earth; the spouse to whom you once had bound yourself in marriage, of your own free will, for the duration of this mortal life.

Yet here you will not get to feel the last of those effects until you have discarded your material form and, in your spiritual organism, strive to raise yourself to the sublime domain of everlasting union with the spiritual counterpart from whom you had been separated long ago; be it that you had already found your other self in this existence, or that another human spirit had been your companion in your married life on earth.

AND IF ALL THE KINDNESS you extended in your marriage is repaid with only grief; if all your patience and good will cannot elicit understanding, your efforts still are not in vain; for in your hands you hold the power to forge the karma that you want; nor can your mortal counterpart in any way deprive you of the inner form that you created for yourself.

All good things you do for your companion here on earth, you will have done them also for your own eternal spouse, with whom you one day shall be reunited to share a single life within the Spirit's world. And here it does not matter whether you are married to your spiritual counterpart already in this present life, or rather to a human spirit that may not find its own eternal other self for ages without end.

"Marriage" in the highest sense prepares the separated individuality for its bipolar form of life in the eternal realm, where both the male and female poles within the human spirit shall be reunited.

Not by fleeing, like a coward, from the problems that attend this preparation, but by your efforts to surmount them will you come to reach the highest form of conscious spiritual life that mortals can achieve on earth.

At this point, I would also cautiously make mention of the mystery surrounding man and woman, even in the physically experienced integration of their opposite polarities.

What crude carnality between two human animals can denigrate to brutish rut—the same can also hold the key that opens the most secret portals of the soul and leads to the sublimest sanctuary.

Like fire, which can furnish light and warmth, but also ravage house and home, so may the energies of sensual desire become transformed to winged steeds before the Spirit's chariot in triumph—provided they are reined by an enlightened "charioteer"—but they can likewise turn into demonic forces of destruction.

Only if the union of the physical polarities is consummated in the highest light of spiritual love can it release the timeless inner powers which lie dormant in the human being's mortal organism.

Then, however, such a union can create a "miracle" that every time anew approaches spheres of highest inner life. And those who witness this event will jointly grow aware of their own selves in spheres of spiritual perfection which no poet's fancy could envision.

I am not at liberty to treat this topic any further.

For those who are mature enough to tread this holiest of earthly paths without inviting danger, a hint will be sufficient to guide them to the heights of this transfigured goal.

But all who read these words should strictly search themselves to be quite certain they are worthy and prepared, in purity of heart and soul, to enter this most sacred shrine within the temple of material nature; for nowhere else are desecrators of things holy punished more implacably than here.

Marriage constitutes the union of two spirits and two mortal natures, but in their bodily existence man and woman are endowed with the potential of a spiritual power that even "gods" might look upon with envy.

The goal that you shall reach one day is spiritual "wholeness," experienced in the union with another spirit that is "whole." Considered thus, your present form of life is but the self-expression of a "part."

Your efforts to transform yourself and gain that inner "wholeness," will be greatly strengthened through the hidden force at work in marriage, if you will learn to use it.

Marriage, to be sure, is also founded for the sake of children; but children, in the end, are not by any means the highest purpose and fulfillment of a marriage.

The fact that you were able to beget and bear a child does not provide assurance that the external life you share is in reality a marriage.

Only where two individual polarities, who in this present life are separated from their spiritual counterparts, earnestly resolve to recreate a new bipolar unity will such a union truly be a marriage.

There is no doubt that children born into a real marriage also find in it the very safest haven and protection. Even so, the purpose of a marriage is not confined to merely furnishing another generation with mortal life and limb, with shelter, food, and education.

Above all else, a marriage is to be a source of inner growth for those who found each other willing to be joined in married life.

Let your marriage be a bond established for each other's sake. Your child, however, should remind you of *the debt you owe the future.*

CHAPTER FIVE

CHILDREN

EACH AND EVERY HOUR human souls are born on earth; and yet, today as in humanity's most distant past, a feeling heart is awed by the event as by a sacred mystery.

Physically, the newborn human enters life the way all animals are born; and just like these it leaves its mother's body, through which had been prepared the earthly form for its external life.

Still, even the most blunted mind is shaken from its torpor for a moment in the presence of the ever pristine wonder when it sees a creature of its kind behold the light of day, and when it for the first time hears its cry.

Very soon that new arrival will reveal its own distinctive consciousness, and parents are amazed to witness the emergence of an independent will, which, although it seems to have its origin in them alone, is now determined to assert its own existence; no matter how unfit the methods might appear through which the infant's will attempts to deal with its surroundings.

In the end, however, the observer must acknowledge that such means are finally the only fitting ones in that they always prove entirely consistent with the faculties the newborn has already learned to exercise.

With each new year of life one then observes new revelations of this growing will, new ways in which it covets recognition, and finally we look upon a grown-up human like ourselves. And often we must then concede that this new person is endowed with spiritual energies that we ourselves could never hope to master.

But marvel follows marvel without end if ever one reflects with open eyes upon a single link of this mysterious chain. And every further cycle of new life creates still more such marvels, which often leave the witness at a loss because he finds himself incapable of comprehending what occurred, revealing tendencies both good and evil.

Indeed, you shall not ever solve the mystery that questions you through children's eyes unless you are prepared to recognize that what lies here before you is something wholly new and individual.

You see too much of your own nature in your child; you let the physical resemblances, which you can recognize, too easily deceive you; you also find yourself and your own traits both in the talents and shortcomings of your child, and thus you feel inclined to see all that reflected likewise in the *spiritual* individuality which, in the body of your child, has placed its life into your hands.

To be sure, the mortal form in which you see your child on earth originated in your body's cells and blood, and thus you pass on to your child a physical inheritance accumulated through the centuries.

As part of that inheritance your child receives a wealth of energies that you believe are "spiritual," not being yet aware of the abundance of mysterious powers inherent in the human being's *mortal* organism. These physical energies, however, are the real agents that transmit the various traits that often lead you to detect too much of your own person in your child.

Embodied in this mortal form, upon whose subtlest powers it is learning how to play, as though it were a harp, there dwells a conscious *something* that is not of this material earth.

It is this *something* you see gazing at you through the infant's eyes as it is searching to detect the same mysterious *something* also in yourself. Perhaps it has already come to be your mortal organism's sovereign master, although it normally is overpowered and enslaved by the material body's restless drives.

This *something* is the *spiritual* human being, which merges with the mortal creature here on earth, creating one of the eternal human spirit's lowest emanations. And in this form the human spirit finds "redemption," earns "salvation," only if it can subject the mortal creature's instincts to its timeless will.

That spiritual human essence is not a trait your child inherited from you, however great a debt it well might owe you for what it did receive in the unique configurations of its mortal brain.

The spiritual human in your child descended from the same exalted regions as the human spirit in yourself. Perhaps you never recognized that spirit as your real self, but suffered it to be so thoroughly oppressed by your material body's energies that you no longer even sense a trace of its existence. And so you think your timeless self is nothing more than just those subtle forces of your external organism which, in the majority of human mortals, have usurped the place of what should be their *spiritual* self-awareness.

It is that timeless human spirit whose searching gaze examines you when you behold your child; even though its eyes are not yet practiced tools as it is striving to discover whether its own kind might still be found on earth in freedom from material chains.

Here you thus have every reason to look upon your child with reverence—unless the human spirit in yourself is sovereign master of your body's subtle forces—for through that infant's eyes its spirit watches you in its primordial, undeflected purity.

Its earthly fate is now entrusted to your hands.

It thus depends almost entirely on you whether this embodied human spirit, which never lived on earth before—unless it were one of the rare exceptions I discussed in other contexts—and which will not return to earth again, a spirit which, in every human individuation, manifests itself as a unique identity, will be able, in your child, to subjugate and freely master what you bequeathed to it as an inheritance received in its material body.

If you are so enamored of your person and your kind that also in your child you only want to find yourself and your own line, then your conduct will give little promise that the newborn human spirit, which put its fate into your hands, can truly learn to master all the things it must subdue.

But under cosmic law you never have the right to turn your child into a mirror of yourself, because the highest and most sacred essence which reveals its presence in your child is infinitely more sublime than all the treasures it received from you as a material legacy.

YET THERE IS MORE INVOLVED than even that; for both domains—the spiritual and that of earthly nature—remain connected through the human soul's dynamic elements. These elements of innate will were formed by human mortals in past ages, but did not reach their full development in earlier human lives and, thus, are now determined to achieve that self-expression—through your child's potential.

These elements are likewise not a legacy your child received from you.

You cannot recognize the human beings who were the "forebears" of your child concerning this inheritance, unless the living spirit in yourself already is unquestioned sovereign and integrated with yourself as *one*, so that it could allow your eyes to "see" what mortal vision is not able to perceive.

You have no right to claim the elements that form your child's eternal soul—elements that may endow it with outstanding gifts—as traits imparted by your mortal flesh and blood. Nor have you any right to shackle, let alone suppress, whatever elements your child possesses which are in conflict with your wishes.

The rights you have in dealing with your child are narrowly defined by cosmic law.

Your only rights are those accorded to a host who has the honor of providing shelter and protection for a noble guest who is prevented, at the moment, from seeing to his own defence.

Everything you do in "bringing up" your child ought to be guided by this insight, lest you should act badly, even in good faith, despite your best intentions.

A human spirit has sought shelter in your care; a spirit whom you furnished only with a body, as the dwelling that should serve it here on earth.

This guest arrived with his own treasures; he did not take his wealth from you.

What he expects from you is only that you nourish and protect him, and that you will support his efforts to secure, within the house you built him, the servants that he needs in order to assert his sovereignty on earth.

I KNOW FULL WELL THAT such advice is not what those would like to hear who seem to think their children's very life and death is subject to their whim and pleasure.

Also some professional "educators" are bound to toss this book aside in "righteous indignation."

The latter may consider that I am quite aware that frequently the children they are supposed to form, instruct, and educate have long since been deformed and scarred by strict parental "discipline."

I here address myself primarily to parents raising their own flesh and blood, and I am speaking of the child that has not yet been robbed of its inherent and integral rights, owing to its parents' false conception of their "powers." The child, in short, who does not yet seek vengeance of the kind each child is bound to practice who feels its spiritual nature strangled, through its parents' fault, and senses the dynamic forces of its soul enslaved by servitude to earthly flesh and blood relationships.

YOUR CHILD CAN GUIDE you as a wise and helpful teacher if you are able to discern how its eternal human spirit constantly attempts to penetrate the many veils of the material form you gave it as a body.

Your child can be far older than yourself, by virtue of those elements within its soul which gained their drive in distant ages. These elements are now combining in your child in a unique configuration, seeking to attain fulfillment in a permanent identity, unified within and through that human being's timeless will.

You ought not to expect your child to "honor" you if its horizon far exceeds your own.

Do not assume that you can simply force your child into whatever mold you please because it still is unaware of its inherent dignity and value as a person—and that there is no price to pay for your transgression!

Concealed within your child there is a witness from whose eyes no deed is ever hidden.

Far more indelibly than you imagine will that witness register each glance you cast, each word you utter. And though your child must outwardly obey your will, you nonetheless shall be defeated in the end if the obedience you enforce is not exclusively required for the child's own good.

Your arm's superior strength gives you no right to bar a human soul, which owes you nothing but its body's life and outward form, from its inherently determined course and force it on to paths decided by your will.

The Spirit's law will in the end inexorably claim its due.

If you have sinned you should not be surprised if your misdeeds shall one day come to light and bear a bitter harvest.

On the other hand, the more attentively you honor the divine scintilla which, in your child, has placed itself within your hands, the more distinctly will you also sense again the same divine scintilla in yourself. And thereby, as your own child's pupil, you well may learn how to discover that scintilla in your own eternal soul.

You then will comprehend what the divine Anointed meant with the much quoted words of his advice that those who sought to "enter into the kingdom of heaven" must first "become as little children."

It is not wealth and knowledge, nor the formal "education" you may give your children to support them on their way through life which they shall later look upon with gratitude, but only that you had allowed them to become the human individuals through whom their spiritual nature was able to express itself.

In homes where several children, born of the same parents, are growing up together, they sometimes will be treated, without thinking, like cuttings from a single tree. And yet, for one whose inner eyes perceive the worlds of Spirit, there are not seldom greater differences separating siblings than there exist between two strangers from nations of a different race.

But not the revelation of the individual human *spirit* only is unique in every child, and thus distinct from every other child on earth; for equally unprecedented are the elements that form each human spirit's *soul*—like crystals that arrange themselves around a common center—producing in each case completely new configurations. And some among these elements may have been formed through human lives of many earlier generations.

A GIVEN CHILD MAY HARBOR elements within its soul whose impulse had been generated by a mortal born in far-off regions of the earth.

Another child may be endowed with elements, at work within its soul, which owe their primal impulse to a human being's will whose earthly life was spent before the pyramids' foundations had been laid.

Within the soul of yet another child there may be elements astir whose impulse stemmed from someone who was forced to leave this life against his will, or may have died a martyr's death for his conviction.

In a pauper's dwelling may be born a child whose soul embodies elements inspired on a throne, while in a rich man's child a soul may seek expression that bears the imprint of a tramp.

And even the same parents' children may display all these divergent elemental forms, shaped by long forgotten generations, in countless shades and combinations.

THE TASK YOU FACE will not be to prevent—by dint of "iron discipline" and outward force—such traits within your offspring's soul as you attribute to destructive tendencies from all expressions of their nature; for what you might achieve that way will always prove illusion; even if, in later life, your child might rise to high positions of respect and fame and thus may cause one to forget what nonetheless remains alive within its soul.

Instead, you ought to make it your concern to steer those energies into a different direction; so that, from childhood on, they find the self-expression they demand, but in pursuit of goals that never could be harmful to your child, nor damaging to others.

Many a family's good name could have been spared disgrace had one but taken pains, at the first inkling of a child's unwholesome traits, to "redirect," with patient empathy, its soul's less beneficial elements, and had these been diverted into channels where they could manifest their powers without creating harm.

One carefully will have to weigh, considering the circumstances of each case, what kind of "redirection" might prove the most effective.

But do not let appearances deceive you!

A drive's inherent power has not been extinguished if only fear of punishment prevents it from expressing its true will.

Nor, for that matter, should one purpose to destroy those elements within a human soul which one considers undesirable; for each such element is, in itself, by nature "good," and, having been directed towards constructive goals, can be transformed into a genuine blessing and thus contribute to a soul's perfection.

So FAR I ONLY SPOKE OF elements that form the human soul whose motivation was instilled by low, destructive will, and which express themselves in conduct that is not desirable.

But you may possibly consider "undesirable" even inclinations, created by the soul's dynamic elements, that owe their impulse to a lofty spirit, far removed from any evil, merely because the elements that would gain form in *your* eternal soul react to them as to a foreign, hostile influence.

You wish to see the inclinations you create yourself gain visible expression also in your child. Instead, you recognize that what is active and alive within your child are energies that stem from a completely different source.

The sacrifice that is expected of you here is self-denying, wise renunciation, even if this act is bound to be quite painful; but otherwise you would commit a grave offense against your child's incarnate soul.

PERHAPS YOU HAVE FOR years enjoyed imagining the things your child might some day be, and have already carefully prepared each step of its career.

And now you see the castles you had built with best intentions being rudely toppled and demolished by your child's own native gifts, to which, in fairness, you cannot deny respect.

Here it must reveal itself whether what you claim to *love* is in effect your child—this wholly new, unprecedented human individual that now must learn to live its own life here on earth—or whether, unaware of your misled affection, you never truly loved your child, but rather your own person, whose reflection you admired in your child.

The decision may be hard indeed, but if you would act wisely, and in accordance with eternal laws, you must be able to forget and bury your ambitions, in favor of the love you bear your child.

Nature chose you as her mediator of a mortal life on this particular earth, in order that the human spirit's timeless truth might here reveal itself, in forms of infinite diversity, in order to be able to "redeem," to free itself again from its desired striving toward the dark in realms below.

Help nature to accomplish that intent! And, thus, help all humanity within the Spirit's world, which let you furnish it with a material body, born of your own flesh and blood.

And in this way you also shall most actively "redeem" the human spirit in yourself, and thereby help it to achieve its own "salvation."

You thus will find your children guiding you: to your own self—to your eternal Living God—and to the Life that has no end.

AND IF YOU DOUBT MY saying that the mortal body is, in truth, the only thing your child receives from you, I must remind you of the fact that many things are commonly ascribed to *spiritual* powers which have their real causes purely in the energies embodied in man's *mortal* form.

For the development of those material, subtle forces, which your child is able to inherit, forces that are usually mistaken for authentic spiritual faculties, it is, indeed, of critical importance whether the eternal human in yourself already gained unchallenged domination, or whether you are still a thrall to instincts of your creature life.

Even so, the energies through which your child receives from you all of its gifts and talents are, in truth, of purely *earthly* nature.

Endeavor, then, to make this earthly heritage a legacy your child can truly bless.

CHAPTER SIX

THE HUMAN BEING
OF THE AGE
TO COME

As long as humans on this planet shall live in social groups or states of any kind, there will forever be some individuals who feel dissatisfied with the conventions that bind their lives to others, but humans still shall never find a form of government one can regard as truly perfect.

The advantage gained by one is bound to be the disadvantage of another; and very few shall ever willingly renounce their gain, even if they know full well their actions will harm others.

Here on earth, one never can create a "city of God"—a state that would unite all human beings freely and in selfless love—for man himself had once bereft this world of God, the time when, terrified of his own might, he for-feited dominion of the earth.

However zealously utopian theories might promise "paradise on earth" for all mankind, reality will always scoff at and ignore ideas of wishful thinking.

All "republics" have their "kings" and "princes," nor can any "autocrat" ensure that nothing sub-ject to his power will elude the grasp of his despotic will.

Never shall deliberating bodies of the many contrive a law that could surpass the wise, majestic statutes which long ago great "kings" had given to the world.

Few at any time will ever be endowed by nature with the power of creating order out of chaos, or of guiding all who, lacking prop-er guidance, would not advance their own affairs nor be much help to others.

Fewer still are those whom nature granted the authority to govern as a right from birth, to make them rulers over everything that can or will not practice self-restraint.

ALL DOMAINS OF COSMIC life, whether they be known through physical or spiritual senses, obey the principle of *hierarchy*, of higher and of lower place and function; and as the ruling entities progressively grow fewer, so their powers and the range of their dominion increases in proportion.

The public life of mankind, too, is subject to that timeless law, and any willful disregard that here endeavors to impose "equality," even with the best intentions, condemns itself to failure from the start: is doomed to trudge the path of bitter disappointments which nature holds at all times open for mortal hubris and conceit that still knows nothing of her ancient laws, or foolishly ignores them, despite their being known.

Wherever humans on this earth create communities of any kind, these can be built upon the principle of hierarchy, of individuated ranks and orders, in harmony with nature's law. And where this goal is not pursued on purpose, nature will herself enforce her law, but then without compassion for the casualties which such enforcement may exact.

The laws that govern cosmic life can neither be evaded, nor satisfied in other ways.

BEING BORN WITHIN A royal castle does not, however, make a man a "king." Nor can all the wisdom of a great philosopher, who longs to see the monarch's subjects happy under his enlightened rule, transform a prince into a brilliant leader of his state.

The secret inner force that manifests itself in genuine "kings" may well survive within a given dynasty for centuries. That very force, however, must expire as soon as the distinctive impulses that once had founded "royal" nature in a line have been exhausted and fulfilled through actions in this life. In that event, no might on earth is able to replace by mere external force what has been lost, in order to protect a kingship that has become an empty shell.

Not every "king" who lost his land has thereby ceased to wear a royal crown; and, likewise, many a throne was toppled by a foe of royal might who surely did not realize that he himself was in effect a "king," but one whose realm had not yet found him.

Human faith in *progress*, concerning the development of governmental forms, is certainly a pardonable error; for mortal eyes are only too inclined to see their own confined surroundings as the "world" at large. And, similarly, mortal minds have difficulty in conceiving that the "ages" they are able to survey are little more than seconds on the scale that comprehends eternity.

The few on earth whose faculties allow them to perceive a wider range of space and time cannot avoid acknowledging the bitter truth that—notwithstanding all appearance to the contrary—everything the world regards as "progress" in the art of government of nations amounts, in fact, to pure illusion and that, millennia from now, the human race will still exhaust itself in mindless bloodshed, struggling for the same supremacy of one group or another as it does today; or, for that matter, had been doing thousands of years ago, when human cultures vanished from the earth whose evidence no archeologist has yet exhumed.

At times "the people" will succumb to the illusion that it can be "king"—a ruler who can rule himself. At other times there will be "kings," possessing nothing of true kingship and its mystical authority, who would by force of arms secure the throne to which they have no right. And back and forth the fortunes of mankind will ebb and flow, until the last survivors of the race shall slaughter one another—if spiritual insight cannot still restrain them—given that the last remaining animal has long ago been killed, and every plant already withered under sand and ice. Because this present earth is doomed to perish as a barren waste, while mankind's ultimate "salvation" is destined for a future aeon.

Pity the fate of mankind's final generation; for then the myth of Cain and Abel will be enacted by the thousands, unless that generation will remind itself in time that every fellow human is a spiritual being who would find its own existence also in its neighbor.

Each among the few whom spiritual endowment and transmitted insights have enabled lucidly to apprehend the depth of time and space agrees with me in wishing that even one of those who nowadays, or at a future time, believe they can create a state of lasting bliss on earth might come to see with open eyes what each of us, whom suffering for others has all but turned to stone, must learn to face in undistorted clarity.

Profoundly shocked and filled with shame would such idealists then banish their utopian dreams into the deepest chasms of their soul and never would they seek again to find in mortal life what they had apprehended through their spirit. It is merely their delusion that leads them to believe what they had seen could likewise be created on the little speck of cosmic dust we know as "earth."

THE DREAMS OF SUCH utopian visionaries are nonetheless in some ways full of truth. It is only that the happiness they would create for all mankind can never be attained on earth, cannot be realized by earthly means, nor can it ever, on this planet, be the lot of mortals of the kind they visualize in their imagination.

Let us, then, look forward to a different, a new kind of humanity; one that lives on earth and will enjoy this physical existence, to the extent this present life permits, but which already is far more than merely "of this earth."

We need to guide humanity to a profounder source of happiness; we have to find a well whose waters flow more plentifully—if we indeed would offer brotherly support to those whom fantasies of paradise on earth have turned into committed "saviors of mankind."

We have to rid them of their dreams—and of their notions of themselves—if mankind really is to profit from the truth they dimly fathomed, but then proceeded to reduce to theories of sterile speculation.

Although it is not possible, even for a truly just and honest mind, to guarantee that everyone is granted perfect justice, every human nonetheless can strive for truth and justice in this life; and each can thereby help to counter the present forces of injustice, which even gods could not expunge from life on earth.

THE HAPPINESS THAT mankind truly can attain will be, instead, a happiness of *individuals*. And only in the soul of each and every human being can such happiness become reality.

The new humanity, which one day may arise on earth, will most assuredly not expect that this external world shall grant it lasting happiness. It will, instead, have recognized that the events of outer life are simply what we make of them, and that they can control us only insofar as we allow ourselves to be controlled.

The inner world experienced by the individual must be transformed into a world of peace and quiet joy, and here alone can mortal man encounter happiness that will endure.

How ONE CAN FIND THIS individuated form of happiness is shown the reader through the insights which these books unfold.

That practicing their guidelines can also bring far greater happiness into one's life in this external world, will hardly come as a surprise to those who understand that all existence in this outer world is only the effect of energies that lie *beyond* our physical perception.

One's *inner* life must be the ground from which all things grow forth that are to bring enduring joy into this temporal existence.

The physical, external world is only the dimension of *effects* whose causes have their origin within the soul's profoundest depth.

Those who would improve this present life by making changes in the world outside will only fabricate mirages giving rise to fleeting joy. And what they wrought will soon again disintegrate, because it lacks the inner roots that could sustain it here on earth.

ONE CAN BUT WISH THIS present *Book on Human Nature* might open the eyes of many who today, with best intentions, still wastefully exhaust their energies, committed to the vain belief that mankind's lasting happiness could be created in this present world.

May all whose searching eyes are fixed upon external things, expecting help and rescue to arrive from outer life, at last begin to turn their gaze around—in order to gain *insight*.

When *looking inward* has replaced the search for things without, only then can mankind's life on earth be truly raised to a condition worthy of the human name.

What now are merely hopeful visions of the future can then at last take concrete form; visions that today one still attempts to realize in ways that only risk dissolving their perception into drifting haze.

Humanity of old became supremely expert in forcing this external world to labor in its service. But since its only method is external force, it is in danger of succumbing to the very powers it unleashed.

Mankind of tomorrow will no longer seek to use external force to bring about what it shall learn to realize far more productively by virtue of its inner powers.

Every individual within that new humanity will manifest capacities that far exceed what people of the older mankind had proudly vaunted as supreme achievements of the human mind, unaware within their souls that mortal intellect can never grasp the Spirit, whose all-pervading substance, radiant like the force of lightning, enlivens all creation; the Spirit of Eternity, which neither abstract thought nor scientific instrument can ever press into the human mortal's service, and which derides the phantom "spirit" many thinkers' minds revere—in place of its reality.

Not being prone to self-delusions, I know it is quite certain that the Spirit of Eternity cannot reveal itself from one day to the next throughout the world; for mankind of the waning age has systematically obliterated with its refuse all the inner wells that might have let the present generation find the depth within itself where the eternal waters of creation ebb and flow.

The time will come, however, when these wells shall once more be restored. And those who then are able to draw upon that source will know how to accomplish many things by virtue of the Spirit's power; things that nowadays one still pursues in vain, despite all efforts by the keenest minds.

Even then, however, will this earth not be transformed into a realm of "heaven," and forces raging uncontrolled will always hold the greater part of mankind in their grip.

The new humanity will constitute a realm of spirits called and chosen, and some are even now engaged in founding that reality within.

Perhaps this present generation may live to see the dawn of its effects. But doubtless will the children of our children know about its energies; much as we today have knowledge of the forces which the old humanity believed it had already torn from nature's grip, because it had been able, by cunning and external force, to harness their potential.

The sacred books of ancient times are right in making a distinction between the "children of light" and the "children of this world"— the sphere of uncontrolled external forces— and one who truly spoke with knowledge expressed it very clearly, "The children of this world are, in their manner, wiser than the children of light."

It is greatly to be wished that also the "children of light" would finally grow "wiser," and thus would learn to break the spell through which the "children of this world" still hold them bound and captive.

CHAPTER SEVEN

EPILOGUE

W E NOW HAVE SEEN all paths the human being traveled on its journey.

We saw the human spirit at its origin, when all its life was still imbued with God, and we beheld its "Fall," which drove it from eternal Light.

We witnessed how man's spirit came to be embodied in a mortal creature, and saw it labor in its self-created exile, striving to regain the perfect bliss of its abandoned origin.

We saw the human spirit follow paths that lead astray, but also saw it on the way to Truth. And thus we came to recognize that this material earth can never be the human being's true abode. Knowing this, the great apostle once had rightly said, "All of suffering creation yearns for its redemption through the children of God."

You—THE VERY READER whom I here address— you are yourself a human being, and thus are able to become such a "redeemer of creation," a "child of God," one of the "children of eternal light."

Of course you likewise have the choice—if that is all your heart desires—of finding shallow satisfaction as merely a "child of this world," as one who is held captive by the spell of this material life.

It is you, and you alone, who must decide which path to choose, and nothing can oppose your will if you have once determined your direction.

Perhaps, however, it is precisely making this decision that you find so difficult.

Your highest goal is something you would gladly *like* to seek, but so far you have not been ready to commit your *will*.

If you were able to awaken and direct your will, the joy afforded by that power would make you triumph over all your doubts and hesitation.

THOSE WHO TOLD YOU that the path toward living light was one of endless self-denial, penance, and renunciation have done you grievous harm; for with that kind of teaching they paralyzed your will through fear, and thereby chained it closely to the earth.

But as you see from my disclosures, what you were taught was wrong, because your path toward light need clearly not prevent you from gathering the flowers and delicious fruits that you may come to find along the way.

Indeed, you will not truly learn to love your life on earth until you know that you have found the way that leads you to eternal Light.

Your path to inner light is, in the end, your path to your own self—and to your Living God, who dwells concealed within your soul.

The One I speak of is the *Living God*, not some imagined "god" of mere belief whose attributes idolaters may worship.

It is not difficult to find your Living God if you have courage and will trust him—before you come to *know* him as he is. But ever farther will he vanish from your sight, the more faint-heartedly you first demand some "proof" that he is truly *real*, and that the power to approach him is something you in fact possess.

And so, the more you turn away from him, the more he shall elude you. As a result, you have no choice but to fall prey to that external world, whose forces would obey you if your spirit's life were consciously united with your God.

In the end, it simply is an act of conscious will that offers you the key which can unlock all inner doors that lead to wisdom's secret mysteries.

Even in this outer world you only live within the boundaries your consciousness reveals to your perception. Thus, while many persons may be gathered in one place, each will nonetheless be self-aware not only in profoundly different ways, but in the most dissimilar dimensions of experience that constitute this present world.

You, however, have attached yourself so closely to the life of this external world that you might well regard it as a "miracle" to hear of someone who is able *consciously* to enter a dimension of the Spirit that you can scarcely fathom, because the energies your consciousness perceives are frequencies that differ fundamentally from those which make the Spirit's world a tangible experience to that person.

In your judgment, the outer world around you constitutes definitive *reality*, and only with suspicion do you look upon your inner life, where you believe all things are merely phantoms and illusion.

But also here is true what I have said before: You cannot find the inner world's reality unless you have the courage to trust its very *being*, before you get to *know* it.

Reality will slip the farther from your grasp the more you fear it might delude you, and thus require "proof" of its existence, unaware that real *proof* awaits you only as the crown that shall reward your patient and courageous quest.

YOU CERTAINLY ARE WELL advised and guided by sound instinct if in your outer world you first want proof before you trust, because that world of physical, external things is truly a dimension of appearance and deception; and even what that world calls "proof" is rarely free of masked illusion.

You are so much accustomed to a realm pervaded by deceit, in which you feel you must protect yourself before you act, that you assume the same distrust is justified when you approach the world of *spiritual reality*.

What you call "truth," whose substance you consider firmly based on solid "proof," contains so many crude and subtle fallacies that you have lost the touchstone of objective judgment. And if one leads you to the way created by Reality, and you indeed encounter final Truth, you grow afraid and drive its light away, thinking you are merely haunted by delusions, because your phantom "truth" has long since made you its dependent slave.

EPILOGUE

Before you can experience Truth in its unchangeable reality you need to learn how to pursue it in a new and different way.

A "re-evaluation of all values" would here, in fact, be sorely needed!

Of thinkers, ceaselessly rethinking their own "truth," the world will see no end. And if you want no other "truth" than that which human minds conceive, then you can readily select whichever form of "truth" best satisfies your set ideas and caters to your pleasure.

But if you would discover Truth itself, in its eternal essence, radiant might, and ever new *reality*, then you must pursue it in yourself; for only in your inmost self shall Truth one day reveal her secrets to you face to face.

You then will clearly comprehend the things this book intends to tell you.

In its enlarged edition, which now is in your hands, my aim was to express some passages more clearly, so that no reader could have any doubt how to interpret what I say, but gain from it enduring benefit.

Yet even the most lucid presentation can avail but little if you will not within yourself endeavor to strive for final clarity.

Once you have experienced clarity *within yourself*, nothing in my books will any longer strike you as "obscure"; for what I came to bring you is living Light as such, and all whose *will* desires Light shall here discover what they seek.

I readily concede that in this book I often had to represent realities that are not easy to convey through human words. It follows that such words will not reveal their meaning except to minds that strive to comprehend them.

But if, for instance, someone brought you news of El Dorado, a land where you can dig for gold, it likely would not much offend you if that messenger had difficulty in describing how to reach that distant land—of whose existence you had never heard.

Well, then, I too have in this book described a way that leads you to a "land of gold."

Learning how to read my words with understanding will thus be surely worth your while.

And if you do not lack the courage to enter
gladly on the way I show you, then you truly
will discover, in yourself, the richest land of
gold: a land that shall belong to you alone—
forever.

A FINAL WORD

Spirits who would help each other
Must descend from kindred stem.

The Brothers in the realm of Light,
The counselors who guide you,
Are human beings—like yourself.
Not: stones without feeling,
Devoid of all passion,
Dead to this life.

All goals that impassion
Mortals with longing
We, masters, treat with respect.
But our own eyes discern
The ultimate aim of all searching.

All earthly desires
In error and sin
To us are revealed as
Trackless pursuit of
Beauty Eternal.

And so we prepare
Unmistakable paths,
Willing to guide
Souls gone astray
Safely to Light;
Moved with compassion
Abiding in Love.

REMINDER

"Yet here I must point out again that if one would derive the fullest benefit from studying the books I wrote to show the way into the Spirit, one has to read them in the original; even if this should require learning German.

"Translations can at best provide assistance in helping readers gradually perceive, even through the spirit of a different language, what I convey with the resources of my mother tongue."

From "Answers to Everyone" (1933), *Gleanings*. Bern: Kobersche Verlagsbuchhandlung, 1990.

By the same author:

The Book on the Living God

Contents: Word of Guidance. "The Tabernacle of God is with Men." The "Mahatmas" of Theosophy. Meta-Physical Experiences. The Inner Journey. The En-Sof. On Seeking God. On Leading an Active Life. On "Holy Men" and "Sinners." The Hidden Side of Nature. The Secret Temple. Karma. War and Peace. The Unity among Religions. The Will to Find Eternal Light. Mankind's Higher Faculties of Knowing. On Death. On the Sprit's Radiant Substance. The Path toward Perfection. On Everlasting Life. The Spirit's Light Dwells in the East. Faith, Talismans, and Images of God. The Inner Force in Words. A Call from Himavat. Giving Thanks. Epilogue.

The Kober Press, 1991. 333 pages, paperback. ISBN 0-915034-03-4

This work is the central volume of the author's *Enclosed Garden*, a cycle of thirty-two books that let the reader gain a clear conception of the structure, laws, and nature of eternal life, and its reflections here on earth. The present work sheds light on the profound distinction between the various ideas and images of "God" that human faith has molded through the ages—as objects for external worship—and the eternal *spiritual reality*, which human souls are able to experience, even in this present life. How readers may attain this highest of all earthly goals; what they must do, and what avoid; and how their mortal life can be transformed into an integrated part of their eternal being, are topics fully treated in these pages.

What sets this author's works on spiritual life apart from other writings on the subject is their objective clarity, which rests upon direct perception of eternal life and its effects on human life on earth. Such perception is only possible, as he points out, if the observer's *spiritual* senses are as thoroughly developed to perceive realities of timeless life, as earthly senses need to be in order to experience *physical* existence. Given that authentic insights gathered in this way have always been extremely rare, they rank among the most important writings of their time, conveying knowledge of enduring worth that otherwise would not become accessible.

The Book on Life Beyond

Contents: Introduction. The Art of Dying. The Temple of Eternity and the World of Spirit. The Only Absolute Reality. What Should One Do?

The Kober Press, 1978. 115 pages, paperback. ISBN 0-915034-02-6.

This book explains why life "beyond" is not so much a different and wholly other *life*, but rather the continuation of the self-same life we live on earth. The difference between the two dimensions lies chiefly in the organs of perception through which the same reality of life is individually experienced. On earth we know that life through our mortal senses, in life beyond it is perceived through spiritual faculties, which typically awaken after death. At that transition, the human consciousness, which usually is unprepared for the event, is at a loss and finds itself confused by the beliefs and concepts of its former mortal life. As a result, the new arrival faces certain dangers; for, owing to these mental prejudices, the person is unable to distinguish between perceptions of objective truth and the alluring phantom "heavens" generated by misguided faith on earth.

To help perceptive readers form correct and realistic expectations, that they may one day reach the other shore with confidence and without fear, this book provides trustworthy guidance into spiritual life, its all-pervading structure, laws, and inner nature. Given the unbreakable connection between our actions here on earth and their effects on life beyond, the book advises how this present life may best prepare the reader for the life that is to come.

The Book on Happiness

Contents: Prelude. Creating Happiness as Moral Duty. "I" and "You". Love. Wealth and Poverty. Money. Optimism. Conclusion.

The Kober Press, 1994. 127 pages, paperback. ISBN 0-915034-04-2.

Sages and philosophers in every age and culture have speculated on the nature, roots, and attributes of happiness, and many theories have sought to analyze this enigmatic subject. In modern times, psychology has joined the search for concrete answers with its own investigations, which frequently arrive at findings that support established views. Still, the real essence of true happiness remains an unsolved riddle.

In contrast to traditional approaches, associating happiness with physical events, the present book points to the spiritual source from which all human happiness derives, both in life on earth and in the life to come. Without awareness of this nonmaterial fundament, one's understanding of true happiness is bound to be deficient.

The author shows that real happiness is neither owing to blind chance, nor a capricious gift of luck, but rather the creation of determined human will. It is an inner state that must be fostered day by day; for real happiness, as it is here defined, is "the contentment that creative human will enjoys in its creation." How that state may be created and sustained, in every aspect of this life, the reader can discover in this book.

The Book on Solace

Contents: On Grief and Finding Solace. Lessons One Can Learn from Grief. On Follies to Avoid. On the Comforting Virtue of Work. On Solace in Bereavement.

The Kober Press, 1996. ISBN 0-915034-05-0.

In this book the author shows how sorrow, pain, and grief, although inevitable burdens of this present life, can and ought to be confronted and confined within the narrow borders of necessity. Considered from the spiritual perspective, all suffering experienced on this earth is the inexorable consequence of mankind's having willfully destroyed the state of perfect harmony that once had governed nature. Although the sum of grief thus brought upon this planet is immense, human beings needlessly expand and heighten its ferocity by foolishly regarding grief as something noble and refined, if not, indeed, a token of God's "grace."

Understanding pain objectively, as a defect confined to physical existence, which, even in exceptional cases, is but an interlude in every mortal's timeless life, allows the reader to perceive its burdens in a clearer light, and thus more patiently to bear it with resolve.

While suffering, through human fault, remains the tragic fate of physical creation, the highest source of solace, which helps the human soul endure its pain and sorrow, continually sends its comfort from the Spirit's world to all who seek it in themselves. How readers may discover and draw solace from that inner source the present book will show them.

The Wisdom of St. John

Contents: Introduction. The Master's Image. The Luminary's Mortal Life. The Aftermath. The Missive. The Authentic Doctrine. The Paraclete. Conclusion.

The Kober Press, 1975. 92 pages, clothbound. ISBN 0-915034-01-8.

This exposition of the Fourth Gospel is not a scholarly analysis discussing the perplexing riddles of this ancient text. It is, instead, a nondogmatic reconstruction of the actual events recorded in that work, whose author wanted to present the truth about the Master's life and teachings; for the image propagated by the missionaries of the new religion often was in conflict with the facts. The present book restores the context of essential portions of the unknown author's secret missive, which the first redactors had corrupted, so that its contents would support the other gospels.

Written by a follower of John, the "beloved disciple," its purpose was to disavow the "miracles" the other records had ascribed to the admired teacher. His record also is unique in that it has preserved the substance of some letters by the Master's hand, addressed to that favorite pupil. Those writings are reflected in the great discourses which set this gospel text apart and lend it its distinctive tone.

Given the historic impact of the man presented in this work, an accurate conception of his life and message will not only benefit believers of the faith established in his name, but also may explain to others what his death in fact accomplished for mankind.

The Meaning of this Life

Contents: A Call to the Lost. The Iniquity of the Fathers. The Highest Goal. The "Evil" Individual. Summons from the World of Light. The Benefits of Silence. Truth and Verities. Conclusion.

The Kober Press, 1998, paperback. ISBN 0-915034-06-9.

This book addresses the most common questions people tend to ask at times when circumstances in their daily lives awaken their awareness of the many unsolved riddles that surround the human being here on earth. To be sure, philosophy and teachings of religion have offered answers to such questions through the ages, but as these often draw on speculation, or require blind belief, they can no longer truly satisfy the searching mind of our time.

It is against this background that the present book will guide its readers to a firmer ground of understanding, resting on objective insights and experience. From this solid vantage, readers may survey their own existence and its purpose with assurance.

As this book explains, the key to comprehending the meaning of this present life is, first, the insight that this life is but the consequence of causes in the Spirit's world and, thus, has of itself no meaning other than that fact. And, secondly, the recognition that material life is ultimately meaningless if human beings fail to give it meaning: by virtue of pursuing goals whose blessings shall endure. The nature of the highest goal that mortals can pursue provides the substance also of the present book.

About My Books, Concerning My Name, and Other Texts

Contents: Frontispiece portrait of the author. Translator's Foreword. About My Books. Concerning My Name. In My Own Behalf. Important Difference. Résumé. Comments on the Cycle *Hortus Conclusus* and the Related Works. The Works of Bô Yin Râ. Brief Biography of Bô Yin Râ.

The Kober Press, 1977. 73 pages, paperback. ISBN 0-915034-00-X.

This book presents selections from the author's works that let the reader gain a clear conception, both of the spiritual background and perspective of his writings, and of their extraordinary range and depth. For readers seeking knowledgeable guidance through the labyrinth of speculations, dogmas, and beliefs concerning *final things*, his expositions will provide a source of comfort and enduring light.

And since, from the "perspective of eternity," human beings bear responsibility to practice spiritual discernment, lest they be deceived by falsehoods, readers here will find reliable criteria to clarify their own beliefs regarding mysteries that neither mental powers nor religious faith have ever fully answered.

By showing that objective knowledge of spiritual existence is not only possible, but that attaining such experience is finally the foremost task of human life, these books become essential guides for readers seeking inner certainty, which mere belief cannot create. In this respect it is the practical advice these books provide which is their most remarkable characteristic.

Forthcoming:

Spirit and Form

Contents: The Question. Outer World and Inner Life. At Home and at Work. Forming One's Joy. Forming One's Grief. The Art of Living Mortal Life.

The Kober Press, 2000.

The underlying lesson of this book is that all life in the domain of spiritual reality, from the highest to the lowest spheres, reveals itself as lucid order, form, and structure. Spirit, the all-sustaining radiant *substance* of creation, is in itself the final source and pattern of all perfect form throughout its infinite dimensions. Nothing, therefore, can exist within, or find admittance to, the Spirit's inner worlds that is devoid of the perfection, harmony, and structure necessarily prevailing in these spheres.

Given that this present life is meant to serve the human being as an effective preparation for regaining the experience of spiritual reality, this life must needs be lived in ways that are consistent with the principles that govern spiritual reality; in other words, ought to be lived according to the structure, laws, and inner forms of that reality. To show the reader how this present life receives enduring form, which then is able to survive this mortal state, the book sheds light on crucial aspects of this physical existence and advises how these may be formed to serve one's spiritual pursuits.

THE KOBER PRESS

CPSIA information can be obtained at www.ICGtesting.com
Printed in the USA
BVOW071136250613

324240BV00001B/8/A

9 780915 034079